The Queen Of MORE

Poems by her Sidekick

Poems and Original Artwork by

Julie Chafets Grass

ISBN: 0692053603
ISBN 13: 9780692053607

This book was inspired by my mother.

When she was sad
we climbed into bed
and when she was high
we would fly.

Table of Contents

Meet my mother, the Queen of MORE

Do you remember that cartoon character Wile E Coyote? He runs frantically and joyously, taking you along for the ride. And when he looks down and notices that he has run off the cliff and is just pedaling air, he crashes.

That's what life with my mother was like.

I call my mother **MORE** because she thought and felt and lived in superlatives. She was never 'just hungry', she was *the hungriest she'd ever been in her life*! There was plenty of 'not enough' and a never-ending supply of 'too much', but rarely was there 'just enough'.

Life with **MORE** was intoxicating. Her exuberance was infectious. She had an insatiable hunger, a rich imagination, boundless creativity and a mega-dose of 'too muchness'.

Whether we were cutting out paper ants for our winter picnic under the dining table or sculpting meatloaf into a grand castle with turrets, I was there.

And on gloomy days when she didn't have enough energy to get out of bed or brush her teeth or open the blinds, I was there.

When my mother was **MORE**, I was 'not enough' and when she was empty, I was her sustenance and companion.

MORE was a costly gift with her extreme swings of sadness, childlike playfulness, unquenchable thirst, and her inability to contain herself.

She loved me intimately, with intensity and no boundaries. It has been my challenge to figure out how to create limits even though I often don't want them. I wrestle with longing for the richness that comes from being too close and having easy trespass.

And sometimes I feel myself becoming **MORE**.

Containment

Mother dear,
climb into this jar.
Come on now.
Just suck yourself in
until you are the size
of a tangerine
and roll yourself
off the counter into this jar.
It is a great place to be, Mother,
with its 360 degrees
of window.
Once you're inside,
I will put
a golden lid on top.

Or if you do not choose the jar,
I have a lovely shoebox,
deep and roomy.
Just exhale, breathe out until you are flat
and I will fold you
into quarters
like a tablecloth.
and lay you inside.

And if you choose
neither jar nor box,
I will wish you so tiny
that I can pick you up
with two fingers,
put you in the pocket
of an outgrown jacket,
zip you up
and donate you,
to Goodwill.

Her Mommy Ate Her Up

Once there was a mommy who was very empty. When she talked she could hear herself echo on the inside. She asked her little girl if she could chew one of her fingers. Her little girl gave her a thumb. The mommy smiled and asked if she could eat one of her ears. The little girl turned her head so her mommy could eat up her left ear. The mommy said thank you and went out for a walk.

When the mommy left the house, the little girl was sad. She felt sad to be all alone in such a big house. She kind of missed her thumb and her ear but mostly she missed her mommy. When her mommy came home, she said, I want to eat your elbow now. The little girl was so happy to see her mommy that she pushed up a sleeve and offered her elbow. Yum the mommy said. More! I want a knee and a shoulder and a nose and a foot. And the little girl gave the mommy all of her parts.

Mmmmmm... The mommy smacked her lips.
By dinnertime, the mommy had eaten up every bit of her little girl. And the little girl didn't mind because now when the mommy went for a walk, the little girl was not alone. And when the mommy went to sleep, the little girl was there, too, right inside the mommy.

But while the mommy slept, the little girl had trouble breathing. After all, she didn't have a nose. And she didn't have a mouth to tell the mommy that she couldn't breathe. And even if she could tell the mommy, she couldn't hear what her mommy said, because she didn't have any ears.

Sharing Her Womb

We float in her womb
cramped, because there are two of us
in this small space.
Mother curls like a potato bug
so she can fit
in here with me,
all 5 feet 3 inches of her
in this wee pond
beneath her belly.
I see her, my mother's face,
and she sees me,
both of us tethered buoys
in the warm water.
Our feet tangle
and she whispers,
"we are too tiny
to go out there."

Original artwork by my mother, Carol Chafets Colten.

BM Ditty

MORE sits on the lip of the peach-colored tub,
dressed in a paisley kaftan and amethyst chandelier earrings.
She is reading Freud's theory on the relationship between joyful toilet training and a happy adult sex life.
I balance on the toilet seat with my legs extended and in the most beautiful voice, **MORE** sings:

> *"Come out. Come out. Come out you little bm*
> *oh won't you come out right now?"*

And together we squeeze hands and peer into the toilet bowl. Empty. **MORE** smiles as if to say: well wasn't that a good squeeze and aren't you a wonderful little girl? Then another chorus:

> *"Come out. Come out. Come out you little bm*
> *oh won't you come out right now?"*

We peek. Nothing. That's great, **MORE** assures me, not wanting to give even a hint that I am missing my cue. And so we sing the afternoon away, her anxiety filling the room. Eventually, I poop. **MORE** gives me a thunderous applause and calls my father's office to tell him about our success.

The Museum of Our Feelings

MORE greets me at the door
and proclaims, "Today we shall emote
with charcoal and crayons
on manila paper."
MORE declares *SADNESS*
and we tumble into sadness
tiny faces
droopy mouths
football eyes
and teardrops so real
they wet the page.
We are so so sad
at the kitchen table
with our art supplies
and ginger snaps.

Then **MORE** roars *HAPPY*
and I reach for reds and pinks
making lipstick mouths
that fill the page,
curly hair girls with dogs,
girls with flowers,
girls in windows with velvet curtains
and a round O sun
that squirts joy so big
it spills off my paper
onto mother's drawing.

ANGER **MORE** growls
and I draw black Zs
ink lightning
I want paint on my fingers
to make
faster black
across my picture
pushing so hard
onto the paper
I feel it rip.

Exhausted, **MORE** tapes our creations on the walls
and hangs a sign that reads,
WELCOME TO THE MUSEUM OF OUR FEELINGS.
She charges my father a quarter to get in.

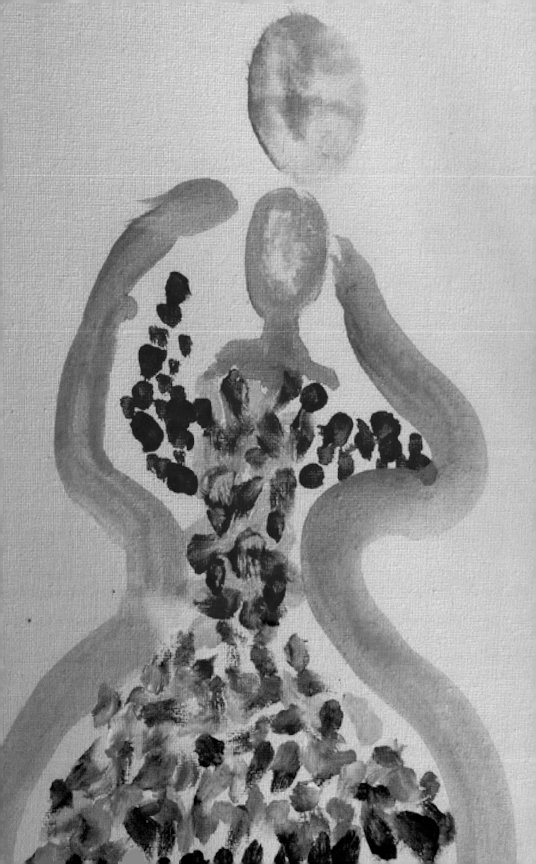

Making Meatloaf

MORE climbs onto the kitchen table,
spatula in hand, and declares,
"Today we are architects, Frank Lloyd Wrights".
She rips off the Saran
and thunks 5 pounds of hamburger meat onto the counter.
MORE and I pinch
and flatten and roll the meat until we build
TADA!
a modern 2-story condominium.
We poke out holes for windows –
make a door out of bay leaves,
squirt the address on with catsup.
When our condo is cooked,
we add sprigs of parsley to create lawn
and arrange endive to make a pond
wide enough to hold a handful of fishy crackers,
with just a splash of ginger ale to make them float.

Our meatloaf is a masterpiece
Julia Child would be proud to serve.

NOTICE
ELEVATOR
— OUT —
OF ORDER

PLEASE
Refrain from
copulating in
the elevator

Midnight Forays

Flashlight in hand,
MORE and I skulk down
cracked cement stairs, no talking,
it's our hush-hush midnight spree
to the Sears chest freezer
in the basement.
MORE digs under the top layer
and pulls out a Sara Lee ready-made fudge cake.
She lifts the cardboard top,
peels down the tin sides
and with furtive smiles,
we take turns
eating all the fudge frosting
off the top
with our pointer fingers.
We keep a roll of paper towels
next to the freezer
to dab ourselves clean
before covering the naked cake
and slipping it back
under icy frozen peas, chicken pot pies,
rib eye steaks and leftover brisket.
Without a word, bound in secrecy
we make our silent climb
up two sets of stairs.
At the landing, **MORE** winks at me
as she turns right into her bedroom
and I go left.

Beyond Splendor

On Easter, **MORE** wraps herself in fuzz,
wears pastels and
strings of jelly beans
round her neck, ankles and wrists.
She eye pencils whiskers across her cheeks
and glue guns a white ball of feathers
on the seat of her pants.
She eats only carrots and lettuce.

I wear my pink leotard
and nestle close to **MORE**
as she watches Harvey
and Bugs Bunny reruns.

Her glee is raucous,
a wild all-consuming hilarity
that mushrooms and spreads
and robs me of the simple
so that my threshold for joy is so high
I can't reach it
even on amphetamines and stilts.

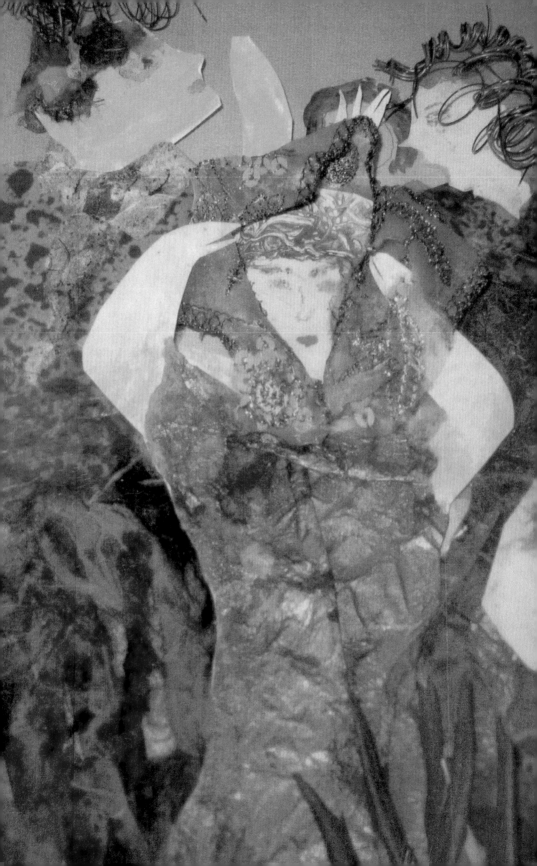

Thanksgiving

MORE is making chopped liver
in the shape of a turkey,
crafting headpieces
of burnished rooster feathers
and only speaking in thee-s and thou-s.
It's Thanksgiving again.
This unhinged pilgrim
dresses in autumnal reds and oranges
with leis of stringed cranberries
and she slogs her way from oven to table,
our ersatz Mayflower,
tethered to a kitchen cabinet.

O how I want
to drift away,
snake through the maze of Herculon couches,
horizontal door turned coffee table,
eight-foot silk ficus trees
planted in Spanish moss-filled sombreros
left over from mother's reenactment of
the War of 1812.

I would wriggle out the door,
down the steps,
so fast I can't hear **MORE**
warbling from the stoop,
"come back thee, thee hast not had thy supper".
I am careening past the grocery
with its harvest frescos and turkey bargains,
wondering how far I can get on thirteen dollars and seventy-eight cents.

Mother is a Mermaid

She rolls down supermarket aisles
in a pink neon wheelchair,
takes languorous naps
in the neighbor's pool,
and christens cans of tuna
in our pantry;
refers to them nostalgically
as Jack, Rita and Selene.

My mermaid sleeps
in the upstairs tub,
I sit on the lip
in a lifejacket;
watch her breathe.
I can't swim.

Chilly in August

I come downstairs
and **MORE** is in her faux fur mink
sitting cross-legged
in front of a blazing fireplace
on a humid, sticky Michigan morning.

Weary of summer,
MORE sets the air conditioner to 55 degrees
and makes cups of hot chocolate
with baby marshmallows and cinnamon sticks.

I climb into the snow pants
she laid out for me,
and burrow under
Aunt Rose Fritzi's patchwork quilt.

MORE gives us winter in August.

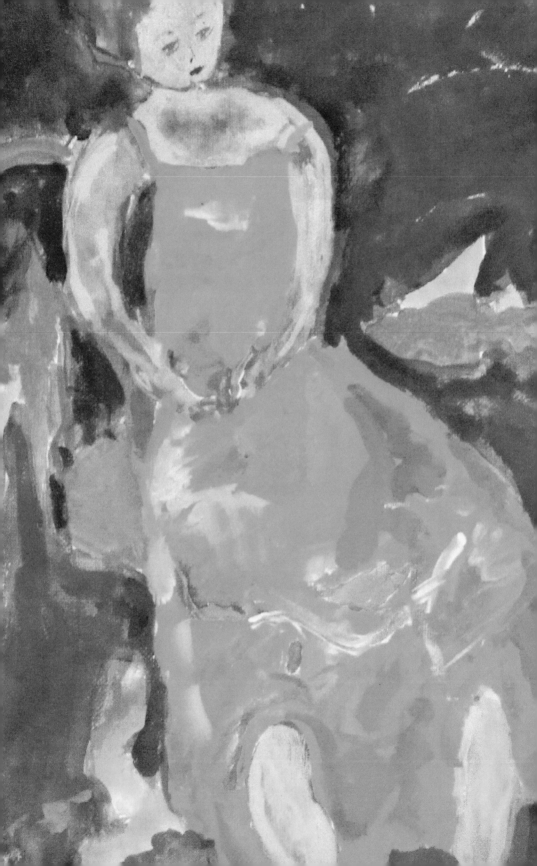

Make-Believe

Today she is a dinghy,
standing in front of the electric fan
in her white silk kaftan.
She billows, puffs up
like a giant sail
in a tempest.
She slides across the wood floor
in athletic socks.

I am a mama trout
wriggling behind her,
gathering my see-through babies
while I swim belly-style
through the living room,
calling,
"Wait boat,
We are tired fishies.
We want to ride on your sunny deck"

"I cannot wait for you little fishy
for I am caught in a miserable storm.
Climb instead onto the rocky bluff
of the sofa and have a little fishy nap.
Your babies will be safe there."
Sailboat is in her room now
moored to the queen size bed,
a mug of gin halfway down the hatch.

Sorry

MORE scolds herself
because she knows
she is feeding her hunger
with my flesh.
It's not good enough anymore
to feel lousy about eating me.
Stop it.
Find some other powerless midge
that can't fight you off–
an ant, a dead bird, your legs.
Eat your own damn legs.

Every morning, MORE asks herself,
"can I do this day?"

Getting It Right

MORE is rehearsing again
on the living room carpet;
legs straight, knees locked,
left hand over her heart,
right on top of left.
Her hair is in a French braid
woven through with rhinestones
in a classic,
eternal do.

I wonder how many hours
MORE spends dead,
while still alive.

Camouflage

Mother is squatting in the geraniums again,
with hunter green socks and Bermudas.
She blooms red above the waist,
even her lipstick
is the crimson of flowers,
her hair swept curly under
a Cardinals cap.

She is half my genetic pond,
this wild chameleon,
who wears gray chinchilla
to commune with the nimbus clouds.

My father is a man
in a black and white photo.
He left me with this mother
who wears saddle shoes
when she visits the zebras.

Her Very Very Highness

When **MORE** discovers
that she is a direct descendant
of Count Eric Stenbock,
the 19ᵗʰ century Baltic Swedish poet,
she buys herself a foot-long,
sparkly cigarette holder.
and a pair of high-heeled, black
boa marabou slippers.

The next day, she greets me
at the door
in her new accouterment,
and pulls me to her bathroom.
She had transformed the entire toilet
into a regal gold commode.
MORE stands beside it
with metallic highlights
in her ebony hair,
an empty can of Krylon spray paint
in her hand.

"I have always wanted to feel like a queen
peeing on a throne."

Loss

MORE, moon-faced
from months of Prednisone,
lung cancer lodged in her brain,
curls into herself
in this steely hospital bed.
I change my baby's diaper,
snap the blue onesie,
look around for a waste basket.
And then I see it.
MORE!
sucking hard on my son's bottle.
Her face calm,
a gentle purr.

I want to snatch that bottle,
to scream,
'You are not a baby.
You are a 55-year-old woman.
You are my mother!'

The wrongness
of Mother chewing
on that rubber nipple,
I can't blot it out.
She hums, self-soothes and
readies to find her space in a womb,
to float in that warm water
without responsibility or pain or desire.
I am too big to slip in beside her,
and even if I could will myself small enough,
my son is in my arms.
I can't leave him.
I can't let her go.

The Funeral

You,
in your pink flamingo casket
lined in aubergine velvet,
propped high on a dead elbow.
You greet me,
a rhinestone cigarette holder
clenched between your teeth,
mylar balloons and paper lanterns.

Mother,
you choreographed this reception
of frog legs and bananas flambé,
Dixie cups teeming with apple cobbler,
and Ella Fitzgerald singing
"When I Get Low, I Get High."

I am here
to celebrate you
O Great Giantess,
to make certain
you do indeed
go down in that box.

I who survived your blonde shag wigs,
black afros and afternoons
cajoling you out of bed
into the shower.
I am here
to say goodbye.

What's Left?

There is a huge sieve
we drop through
at the end of the birth canal.
It catches pieces of us
and holds them back.
The residue settles
in the wombs of our mothers,
to putty up their wounds.
It isn't theft,
just self-preservation.

and

sometimes

I

AM

MORE

Hugeness

I have become this giantess
big woman amazon mother,
rivaling my son's excitement
over a floating soap bubble,
chasing it across the lawn
with my crazed whoops
while his joy shrinks
to the size of a peanut.

What monster
smashes her child
just to have a second helping?

I Suffocate Him

Mother,
you in your giant brimmed hat,
covered with paper machè bananas and plums,
cramming the living room with watercolor nudes
as if we were the Museum of Contemporary Art.
You make pancakes shaped like bears and automobiles.
I want toast.

I smell you when you're not home,
ripe mango in the pillows of the couch.
I fight for oxygen like an asthmatic
when you seep into my room,
blaring orders about socks and bedtime.

Mother, you are too huge for me
with your tapestry boots,
lighting candles at breakfast,
serving cheerios in goblets
like we are dining at the White House.

I need space.
You give me a curfew.

Contain Me

Why aren't you flabbergasted
when you discover me hunched
on the front lawn in my gorilla suit,
zipped up the front,
my fingers pushed deep
into the matted, pleather hands?

En route to the movies,
you have the tickets in your pocket
and I cradle a dozen bananas to my rubber bosom.
Belting me in to the front seat of the Volvo,
you mention that we're out of milk
and turn on the radio
to catch the final score of
the Phillies/Dodgers game.

Do you not notice
that I am dressed like a primate? I smack my chest and make grunting
noises,
curl my legs up and scratch my head with a foot.
Still nothing, but you add 'butter',
we also need to buy butter.

And when we climbed into bed last night
and I pulled down the quilt to reveal
the entire Gettysburg Address
printed with permanent marker
on our ecru sheets,
you took your cholesterol medication and fell asleep.

It all tastes the same. It all tastes the same. It all tastes the same. It all tastes the same.

I've always wanted a red dress with feathers. I've always wanted a red dress with feathers.

Corral me, enjoy me or gather me up
long enough to still me. I am
spinning wild tornado frenzy,
my mind clogged with Czechoslovakian glass,
butcher shops, mountain goats.

Stop me.
In the morning, sometimes my feet disappear,
my hair turns to string
and falls long to the ground.
I am safe in the spaghetti of my head
and I sleep.

Julie Chafets Grass has six brightly painted mannequin feet walking across her kitchen ceiling and she has a gorilla suit in her front closet.
She is an expressive artist, a poet and has a creative curiosity that takes her on the most colorful adventures.
She keeps M & M's and Tootsie Rolls in her nightstand and glove compartment, but only eats them in the dark.

Julie has published poems in several literary journals including Northwest Review, PoemMemoirStory, 88, Hawaii's Review, Eureka Literary Magazine, and Plainsongs. She reads her poetry at salons, bookstores and other venues throughout Los Angeles.

But I was so little then,
hardly old enough
to cross the street
on my own...

Dedications

This book is dedicated with oodles of love
to my champion and husband, Alan who totally gets me,
MORE or less.

And to my 2 sons Ben and Jon who I am so proud of.
I love the way they move in the world,
MORE or less.

All 4 of us rock!

Acknowledgments

To Dale, my talented, patient and generous hero,
and to Lori who graciously taught me the value of a red pen.

And to therapists, so many therapists who have given me the tools, courage and wisdom to figure all of this out.

Made in the USA
Lexington, KY
21 March 2018